This book presented to:

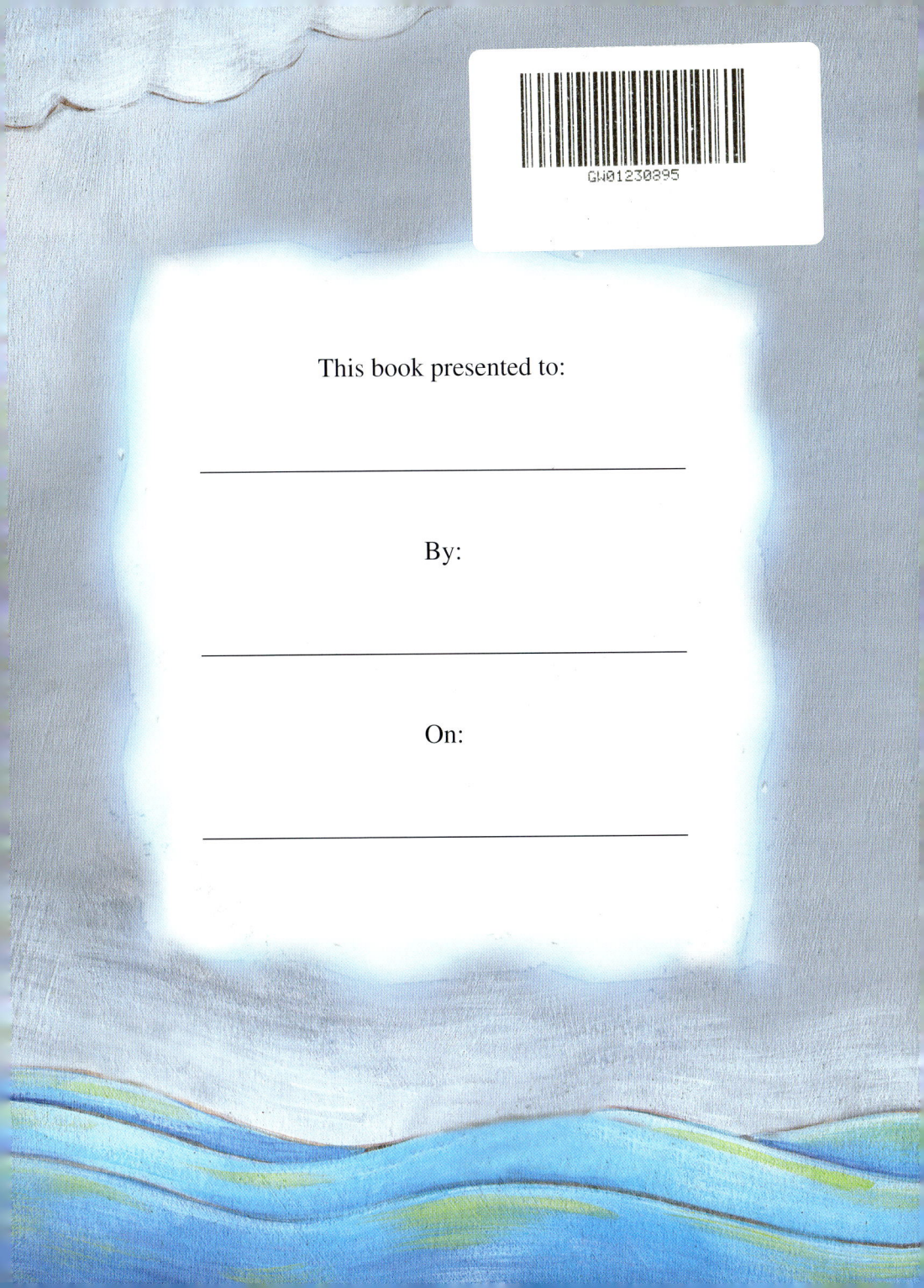

_____

By:

_____

On:

_____

Best-Loved Miracles of Jesus

CONCORDIA PUBLISHING HOUSE • SAINT LOUIS

Arch® Books
Published 2014 by Concordia Publishing House
3558 S. Jefferson Ave., St. Louis, MO 63118-3968
1-800-325-3040 • www.cph.org

Jesus' First Miracle © 1990, 2006 Concordia Publishing House

The Great Catch of Fish © 2006 Concordia Publishing House

Jesus Calms the Storm © 1994, 2004 Concordia Publishing House

Jesus Heals Blind Bartimaeus © 2010 Concordia Publishing House

What's for Lunch? © 1997 Concordia Publishing House

Jesus Wakes the Little Girl © 2009 Concordia Publishing House

All rights reserved. No part of this publication may be reproduced, stored in a retrieval system, or transmitted, in any form or by any means, electronic, mechanical, photocopying, recording, or otherwise, without the prior written permission of Concordia Publishing House.

Scripture quotation from The ESV Bible® (Holy Bible, English Standard Version®), copyright © 2001 by Crossway Bibles, a publishing ministry of Good News Publishers. Used by permission. All rights reserved.

Manufactured in Shenzhen, China/55760/300511

1 2 3 4 5 6 7 8 9 10   23 22 21 20 19 18 17 16 15 14

Table of Contents

Jesus' First Miracle	7
The Great Catch of Fish	23
Jesus Calms the Storm	39
Jesus Heals Blind Bartimaeus	55
What's for Lunch?	71
Jesus Wakes the Little Girl	87

Dear Parents,

People's minds and bodies can do some pretty amazing things. Each new day brings with it news of wonderful achievements and surprising accomplishments. Our imagination allows us to do even more fantastic things. Books encourage us to think about accomplishing the impossible, and movies, with their special effects, show us wild and wonderful scenes that defy logic.

But nothing compares to the real life miracles that Jesus did.

The miracles of Jesus served to show people that He had compassion on them and that He had power over nature. His miracles were the proof people needed to see that He was sent from God and that He was God. And because of that, His miracles confirmed the Scriptures and produced faith.

This collection of Arch Books was chosen to teach today's children about six of Jesus' most familiar miracles. Each story in this collection provides you with context so you can help expand your child's understanding of that miracle and its significance to his or her own life. Our hope is that this collection serves to further your child's Bible literacy overall and strengthens his or her faith in Jesus' Gospel message of forgiveness and salvation.

These [things] are written so that you may believe that Jesus is the Christ, the Son of God, and that by believing you may have life in His name. John 20:31

The Editor

JESUS' FIRST MIRACLE

John 2:1–11 for children

Written by Vivian Dede
Illustrated by Chris Wold Dyrud

The people had gathered.
What feasting! What fun!
A marriage in Cana
Had finally begun.

Many guests were invited,
And Jesus came, too.
Plus disciples and Mary,
It made quite a few!

The disciples and Jesus
Sat down in their places,
But some of the people
Had frowns on their faces.

Then Mary told Jesus,
"The wine is all gone.
The guests have consumed it.
The last jug is drawn."

"Dear Mother," He answered,
"My time has not come.
When everything's ready,
My work will be done."

Mary said to the servants,
"Do all that He asks."
They waited—were ready—
To learn their new tasks.

There sat in the courtyard
Six vessels of stone,
Used strictly for water
And water alone.

Each took 30 gallons
To fill to the rim.
But Jesus instructed,
"Fill each to the brim,

With fresh drinking water."
The servants obeyed
And filled every jug
To the top, as He said.

Then Jesus commanded,
"Draw a cupful at least
To take to the master
In charge of the feast."

The master was startled,
As tasting, wide-eyed.
He went to the bridegroom
And called him aside.

"Most people will furnish
Good wine at the first
When guests are most eager
To settle their thirst.

"But you have surprised us,"
He said with a bow,
"For you have been saving
The best wine 'til now!"

The disciples were awestruck
To see Jesus' power.
It made them believers
From that very hour.

They traveled with Jesus
And helped teach His Word.
And when people came near,
Here's what they heard:

"Believe and be baptized,
Your sins God forgives,
Through Jesus, our Savior.
In peace, we now live."

Dear Parent,

    In ancient times, there was not a large variety of beverages. Water was used for purifying, and people usually drank wine. That is why running out of wine at the wedding in this Bible story was a problem. Weddings were big celebrations and people feasted for days. Not being able to provide for guests was an embarrassment to the host.

    John notes that this event is the first of Jesus' signs, His first miracle. Here Jesus provides for the people, but He did so quietly, almost secretly. Jesus was not eager to make a public display of His divinity. Yet He took action not because His mother asked Him to; Jesus showed His power over nature as its Creator to provide for the needs of the people.

    Also in John 2:4 Jesus reminded Mary—and thereby all of us—that all things happen according to God's will and in His time. Similar expressions are used throughout the Gospel of John (7:6, 8, 30; 8:20). In perfect obedience to His Father's will, Jesus suffered and died on the cross for our sins. His hour had come.

    Use this Bible story to teach your child that God provides all good things, big and little. Then say a prayer of thanks that He provides the most important thing of all—forgiveness of sin through Jesus Christ.

The Editor

The Great Catch of Fish

Luke 5:1–11 for children

Written by Lisa Konzen
Illustrated by Ronnie Rooney

Simon and Andrew fished the lake
Of Gennesaret all night,
But not one fish would their nets take,
So they gave up the fight.

They washed their nets and stowed their gear
As crowds along the beach
Were gathered 'round so they could hear
The words that Jesus preached.

The crowd pressed close to hear His word.
What message would He give?
His words were fresh; they'd never heard
That in Him, they could live.

They listened to Him preach Good News
As water lapped the shore.
When He was done, He told them to
Row out a little more.

"Go out in deeper waters and
Let down your nets; you'll get
A catch of fish so big and grand—
Your best night's fishing yet."

Then Simon said, "We've fished this lake
Without a single bite
But for You, Master, I will take
Another try this night."

They rowed away despite their doubt—
The fishing wasn't great.
They dropped their nets and looked about
But didn't have to wait.

The catch was big; their nets began
To burst and fall apart.
They called to every fisherman
To come and do his part.

The boats began to tip and sink,
The catch was so immense.
It really made poor Simon think
That Jesus' words made sense.

He knelt by Jesus and said "Go
Away from me, my Lord.
I'm sinful and I didn't know
To take You at Your word."

"I didn't trust when You said, 'Fish!'
That I'd find perch or trout.
You gave me more than I could wish.
Oh, Lord, forgive my doubt."

Then Jesus said, "Don't be so scared.
I have a job for you.
So listen up, and be prepared
For what I call you to."

"You see those folks along the shore?
Like fish, they're swimming 'round.
They know life must have something more
Than what they've always found."

"They're looking for a Savior who
Will die to make them free.
I'll give My life, make all things new
So all can live in Me."

Like Simon, we must drop our net
And help those fish inside.
You won't believe the catch you'll get
When in Him, you abide.

Dear Parents,

Simon had worked hard all night and had nothing to show for it. Nevertheless, the exhausted and defeated fisherman obeyed an illogical command from an itinerant preacher. As a result, Simon and his partners were rewarded with incomprehensible success. What they netted was beyond their wildest imaginings. What they netted (besides a lot of fish) was forgiveness and eternal life.

Simon was well aware that he was a contemptible man in the presence of the holy God. Hopelessly tangled in the net of his own sinful nature, he fell to his knees in the smelly, dirty bottom of his boat and said, "Depart from me, Lord, for I am a sinful man."

"Don't be afraid," Jesus told him. "Follow Me." Forgiven, Simon was now ready to respond to Christ's call to serve in the world. He let go of the nets that bound him to his sinful life and put his faith in his Lord.

In addition, the story of Simon Peter's great catch of fish mirrors the great conversion of thousands as they listened to his sermon on Pentecost. Simon had indeed become a great fisher of men.

The Editor

Jesus Calms the Storm

Matthew 8:23–27, Mark 4:35–41,
and Luke 8:22–25 for children

Written by Jean Thor Cook
Illustrated by Chris Wold Dyrud

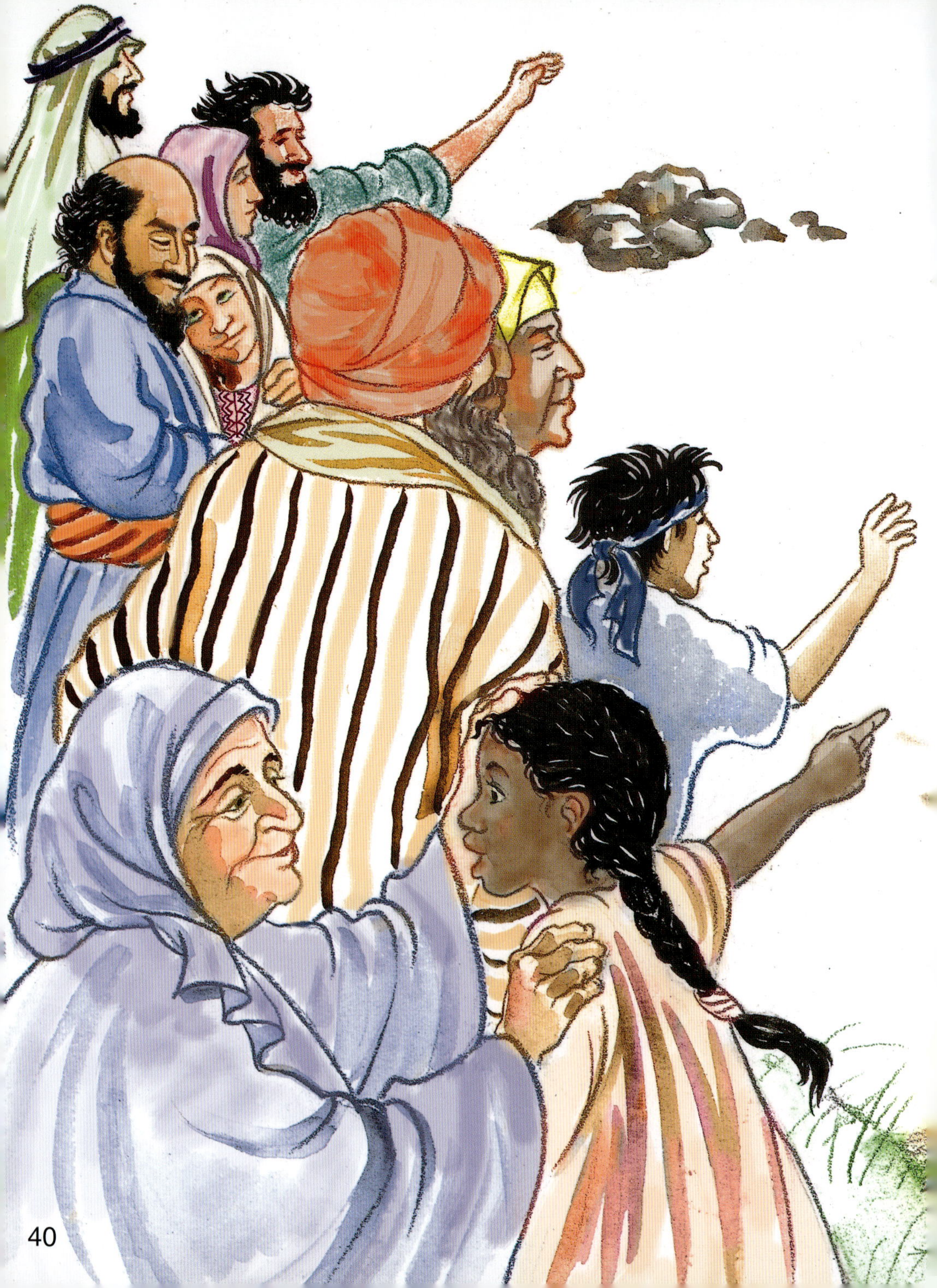

Jesus was tired;
> His hand covered a yawn.
The day had been busy
> From sunrise to sundown.

> There'd been teaching and healing,
>> And stories to tell.
> Many folks brought their sick,
>> And He made them well.

> How could Jesus rest
>> With the crowd still there?
> Why not sail 'cross the lake?
>> The disciples knew where.

The boat left shore.
>The crowd waved good-bye.
Jesus soon slept
>Beneath the starry sky.

At first it was peaceful;
    The waves splished and splashed.
But then a storm came up.
    It came up so fast!

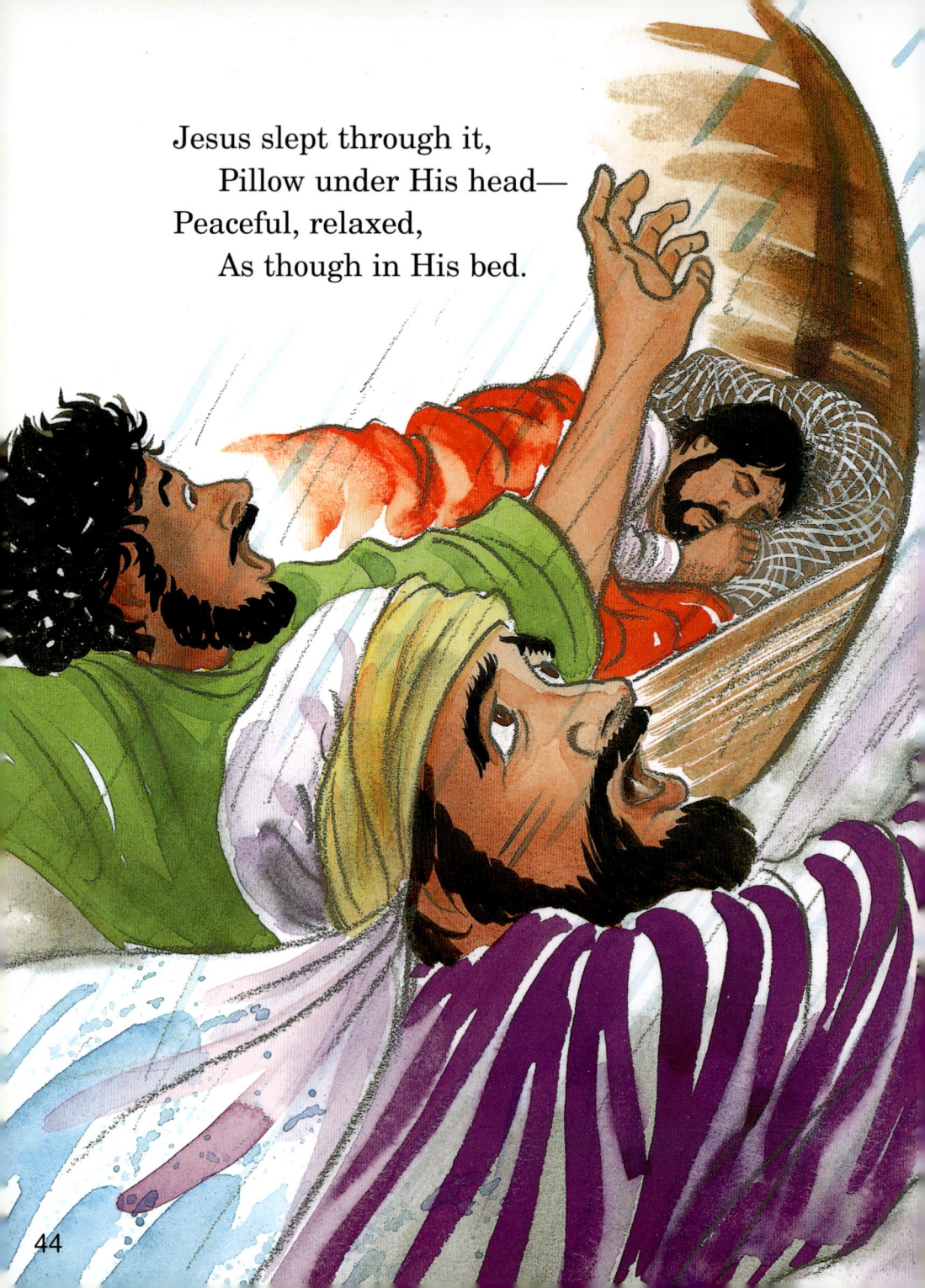

Jesus slept through it,
  Pillow under His head—
Peaceful, relaxed,
  As though in His bed.

The wind shrieked and moaned;
 The boat gathered speed.
Why was Jesus sleeping?
 His friends were in need!

And the winds roared more fiercely.
Waves whooshed o'er the bow.
"We need to wake Jesus,
And do it right now!"

"Don't you know we could perish?"
　　They questioned their Lord.
"Get up or we'll drown;
　　We'll be swept overboard!"

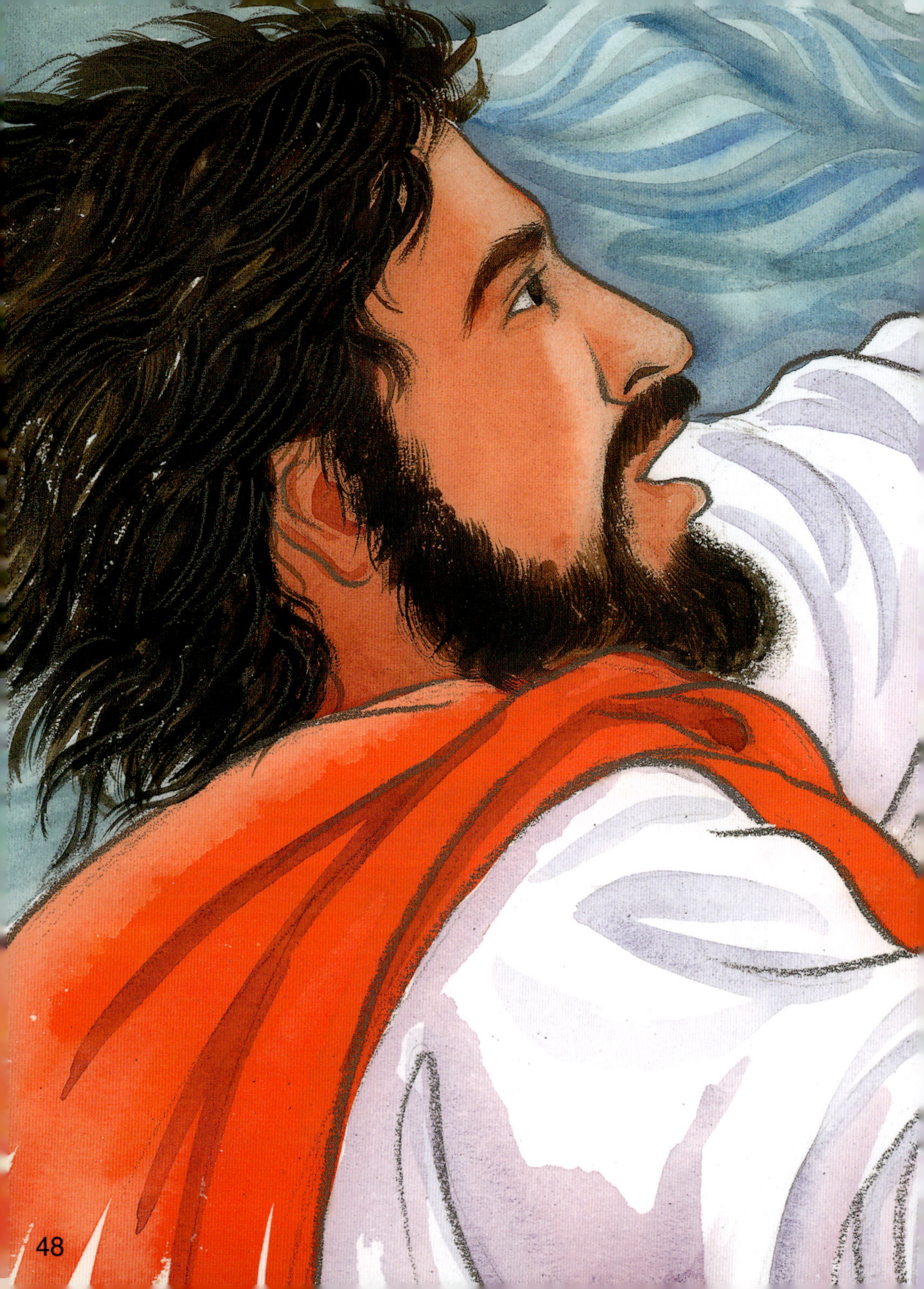

"Be quiet! Be still!"
 Jesus spoke to the waves.
Quickly they calmed—
 They had to obey.

Jesus asked His disciples,
 "Why were you scared?
Have faith!" They'd forgotten—
 Jesus always cared.

The disciples then wondered,
Who was this great man
Who brought them safe sailing,
Got them out of that jam?

He was awesome! Magnificent!
Full of power was He!
How did He take charge
Of those raging seas?

In time, they'd know Jesus
    Was God's precious Son;
That His life would be given
    To save everyone!

Dear Parents:

After reading this story, you might want to act it out. Fill a pan with water, sail a toy boat on the surface of the water, and blow on it with your child to create a storm. Then stop blowing and watch the storm end. Talk with your child about a time when you have been afraid. Help your child understand that we all feel afraid at times. Then read Psalm 56:3 together, "When I am afraid, I put my trust in You."

Explain to your child that just as Jesus calmed the storm, He can calm our worries and fears and help us handle the problems that trouble us. He carried our greatest fear—fear of eternal death—to the cross and won our victory for us. Pray with your child, thanking Jesus for His loving care and forgiveness.

The Editor

Jesus Heals Blind Bartimaeus

Matthew 20:29–34;
Mark 10:46–52;
Luke 18:35–43 for Children

Written by Diane Grebing

Illustrated by Dave Hill

When Jesus walked upon the earth
Many years ago,
He helped a lot of people.
The Bible tells us so.

Lord Jesus made the lame to walk
And healed many ills.
He even raised a dead man,
As was His Father's will.

So many followed Jesus' steps
To towns all around.
They were awed by His miracles.
His actions did astound.

57

One day as Jesus walked along
Near to Jericho,
He came upon a blind man
Who had no place to go.

The man's name was Bartimaeus.
By the road he sat.
He made his living begging
For coins and things like that.

Blind Bartimaeus had to beg.
It was just the way.
Without sight, he could not work.
He sat there every day.

59

His hearing sharp, he heard a crowd
Pass by on the road.
Bart asked, "Hey! What's going on?"
With boldness he was told:

"It is Jesus of Nazareth,
Walking right past you."
Bart was very excited.
He knew just what to do.

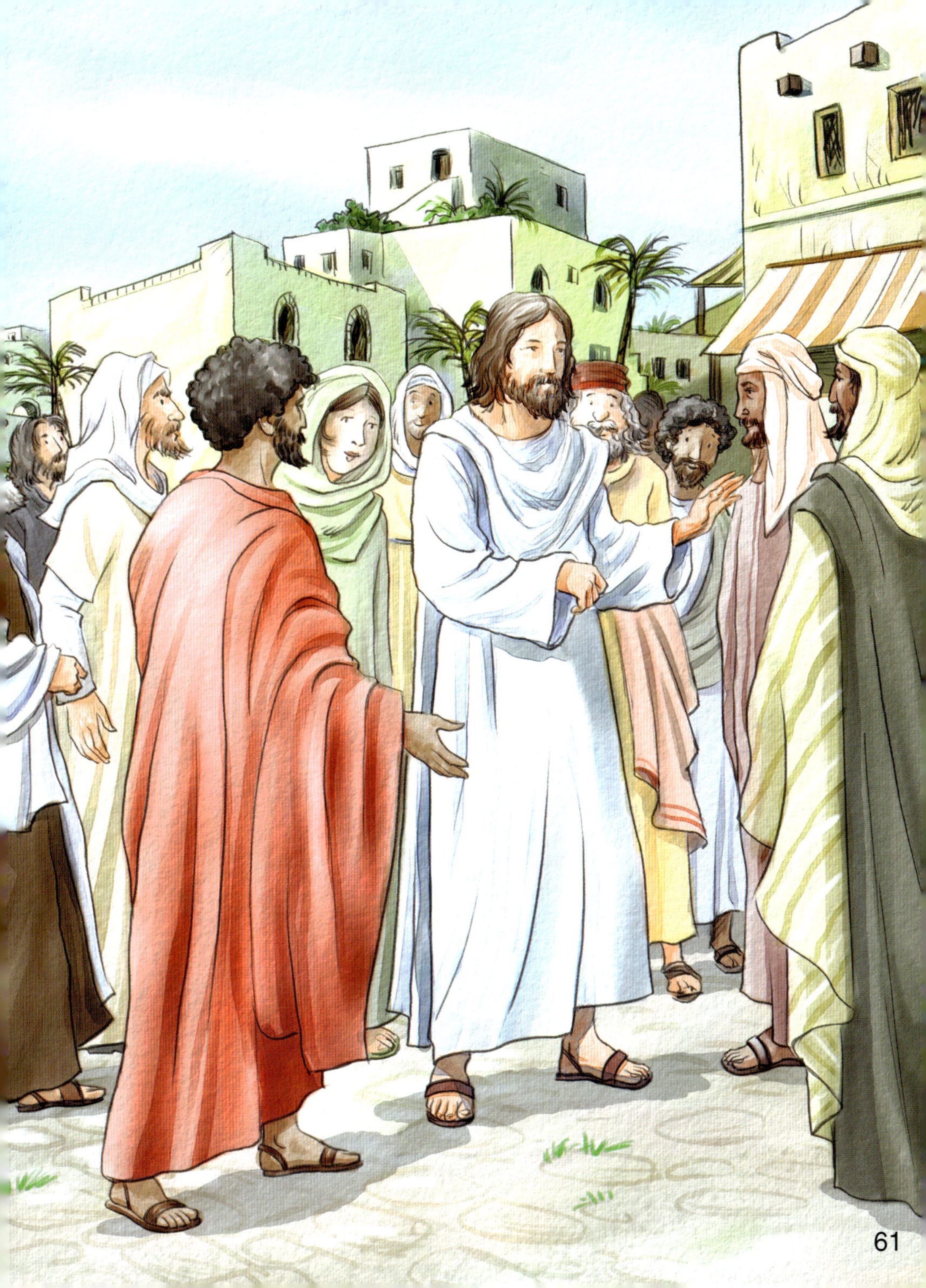

Bartimaeus started shouting
As loud as could be.
"Son of David, have mercy!
Please have mercy on me!"

"Shhh!" said the people around him.
"You are way too loud!"
But Bart kept right on yelling.
He shouted through the crowd.

"Son of David, please have mercy!"
Jesus heard Bart's pleas.
Jesus stopped and commanded,
"Bring the man right to Me."

The crowd shouted to the blind man,
"Up! He's calling you.
Take heart! The Lord is waiting!"
To the ground, Bart's cloak flew!

Bartimaeus rushed to Jesus.
Jesus said, "All right.
What do you want Me to do?"
"Rabbi, restore my sight."

65

Jesus said to Bartimaeus,
"Your faith made you well."
Bart's once-blind eyes now could see!
His heart in thanks did swell.

Then the Lord told Bartimaeus,
"My friend, go your way."
With seeing eyes, Bart did so.
Bart followed Him that day.

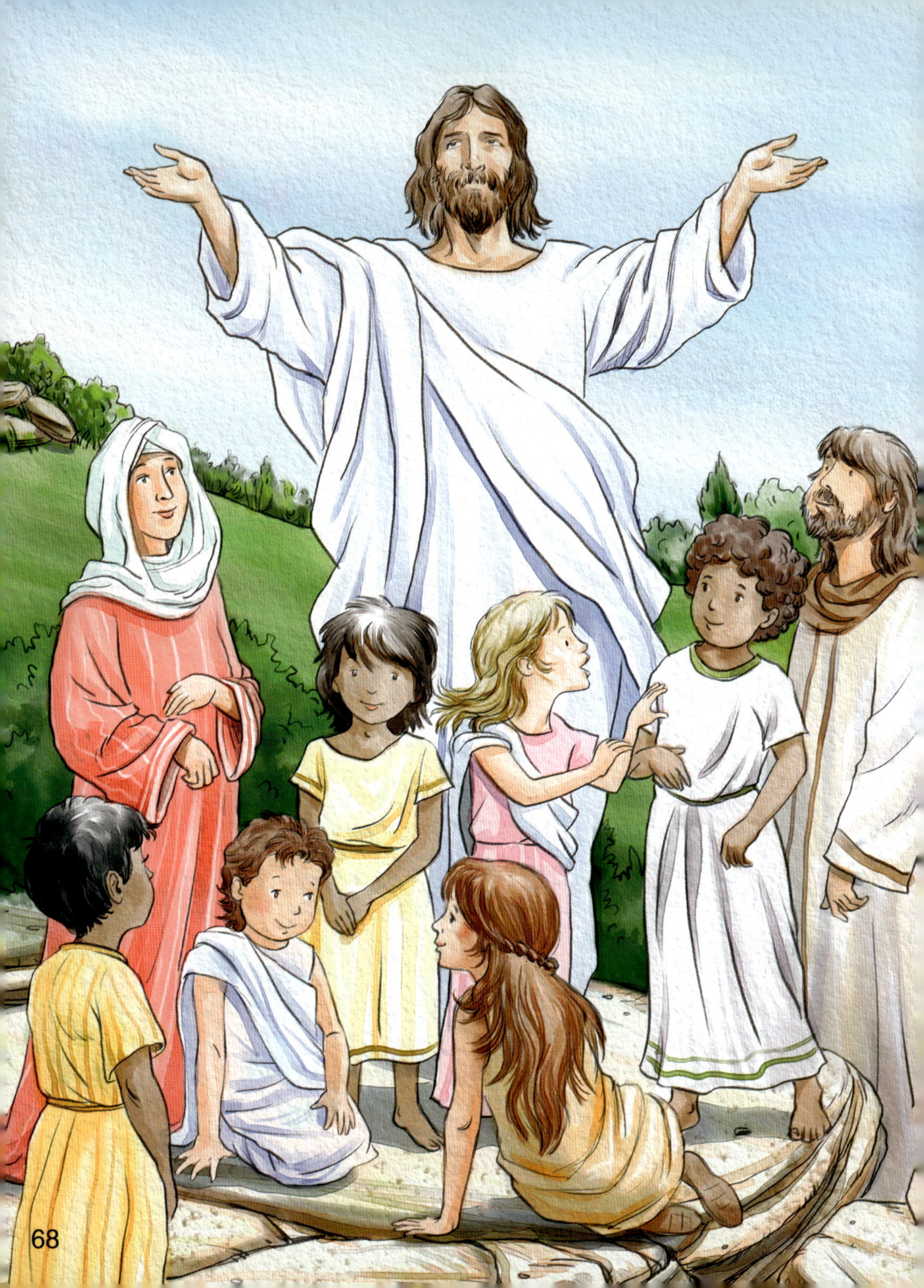

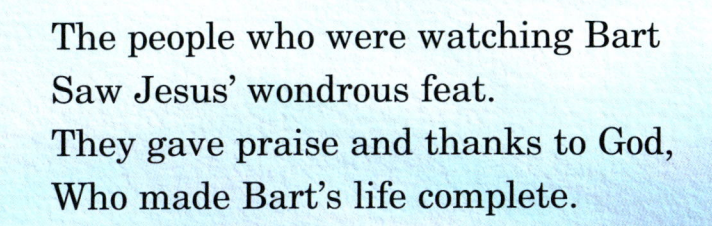

The people who were watching Bart
Saw Jesus' wondrous feat.
They gave praise and thanks to God,
Who made Bart's life complete.

Jesus pow'rfully helps us too.
He leads us to see
Our need for His saving love.
Let's praise Him joyfully!

Dear Parents:

"Jesus, Son of David, have mercy on me!" (Luke 18:38). Bartimaeus cried out these words as Jesus passed by him near Jericho. Having no other hope to be able to see, Bartimaeus asked Jesus to show compassion, kindness, and action toward him. Bartimaeus's request shows his knowledge of who Jesus is and his trust in Jesus' power to help him. Jesus miraculously answered the blind man's plea. Jesus said to Bartimaeus, "Your faith has made you well. And immediately, [Bartimaeus] recovered his sight" (Luke 18:42–43).

We, too, cry out to Jesus to "have mercy on us." There are times throughout our lives when we may need physical healing. Daily, we need spiritual healing because of the sickness of sin. On our own, we cannot clean sin from our hearts. But Jesus can and does! He heals us of all our sins, renews us, and restores us so we can live for Him and follow Him. Jesus does all this, not because we deserve it, but because He loves us! That's His wonderful grace and mercy.

Help model for your child a life of dependence on Jesus. Pray daily with your child. Ask Jesus for help with daily tasks, for forgiveness, and for a strong faith. When troubles occur, ask Jesus for His mercy. Praise and thank Him daily for His love and compassion.

> Thank You, Jesus, thank You
> For Your mercy every day.
> Help us, Jesus, help us
> To follow in Your way.
> Cleanse us, Jesus, cleanse us
> From the sin within our hearts.
> Praise You, Jesus, praise You
> For the power You impart. Amen.

—The Author

What's for Lunch?

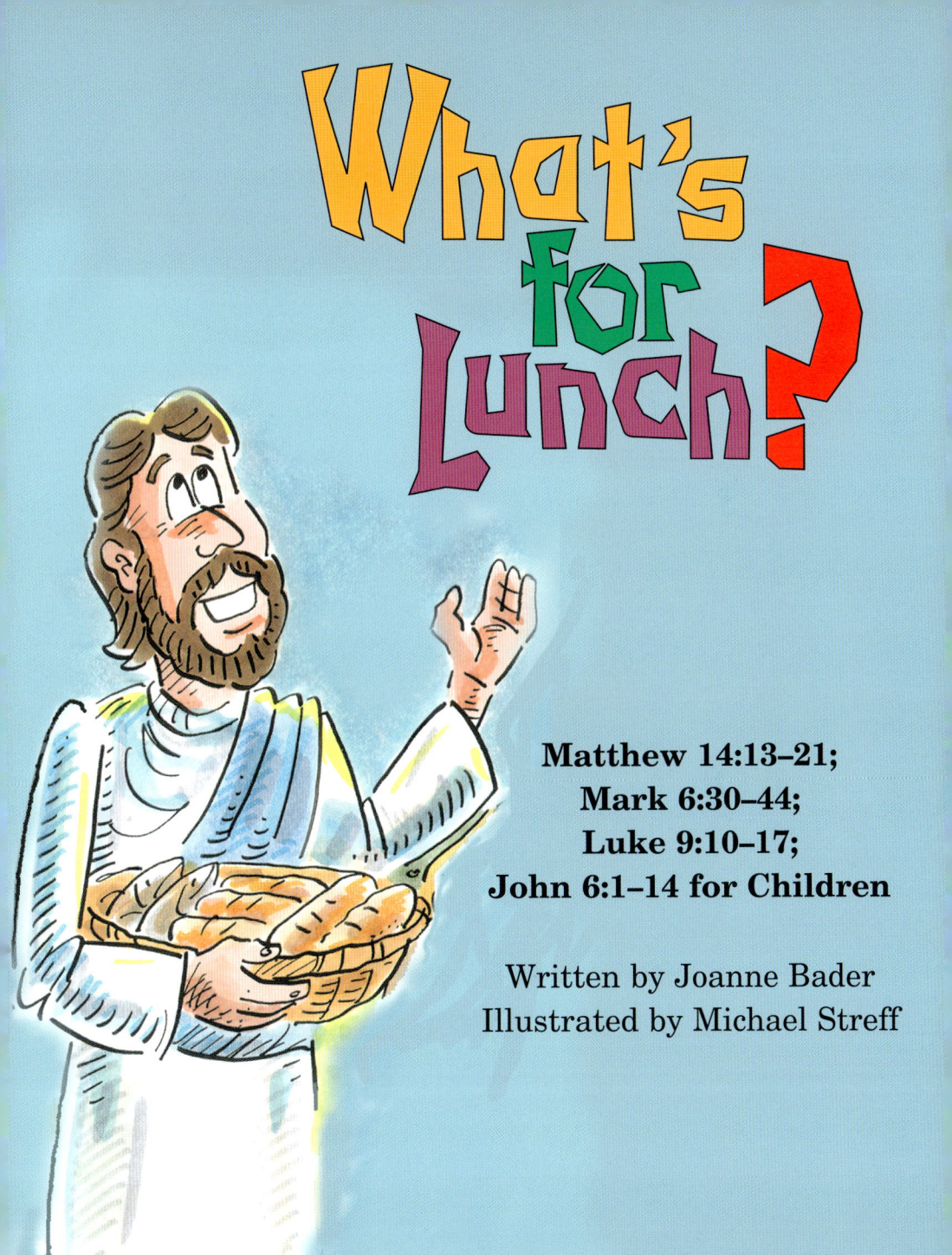

Matthew 14:13–21;
Mark 6:30–44;
Luke 9:10–17;
John 6:1–14 for Children

Written by Joanne Bader
Illustrated by Michael Streff

Jesus and His followers
Had traveled far and wide.
They came across a quiet sea
And climbed the mountainside.

Jesus would have liked to rest
From work that He had done,
But crowds of people followed Him
And joined Him in the sun.

73

The people loved to hear Him preach.
They shouted, "Tell us more!"
Some hoped to see the miracles
They knew He'd done before.

He welcomed them and spoke to them
About the Word of God.
He healed all those who needed it
With just a gentle nod.

When evening came they searched for food,
But the disciples said,
"Let's send them home or into town
To eat and go to bed."

"They do not need to go away,"
Our Lord replied so calmly.
"You give them something they can eat—
For this crowd is quite hungry."

At last one of the Twelve spoke up
To tell what he had found.
He told the others that a boy
Had food to pass around.

"Well, just what is it?" they all asked.
"How many will it feed?
We must do something here and now."
On that they all agreed!

"It's not much food to feed this crowd,"
The one disciple said.
"He only has two fish to eat
And five small loaves of bread."

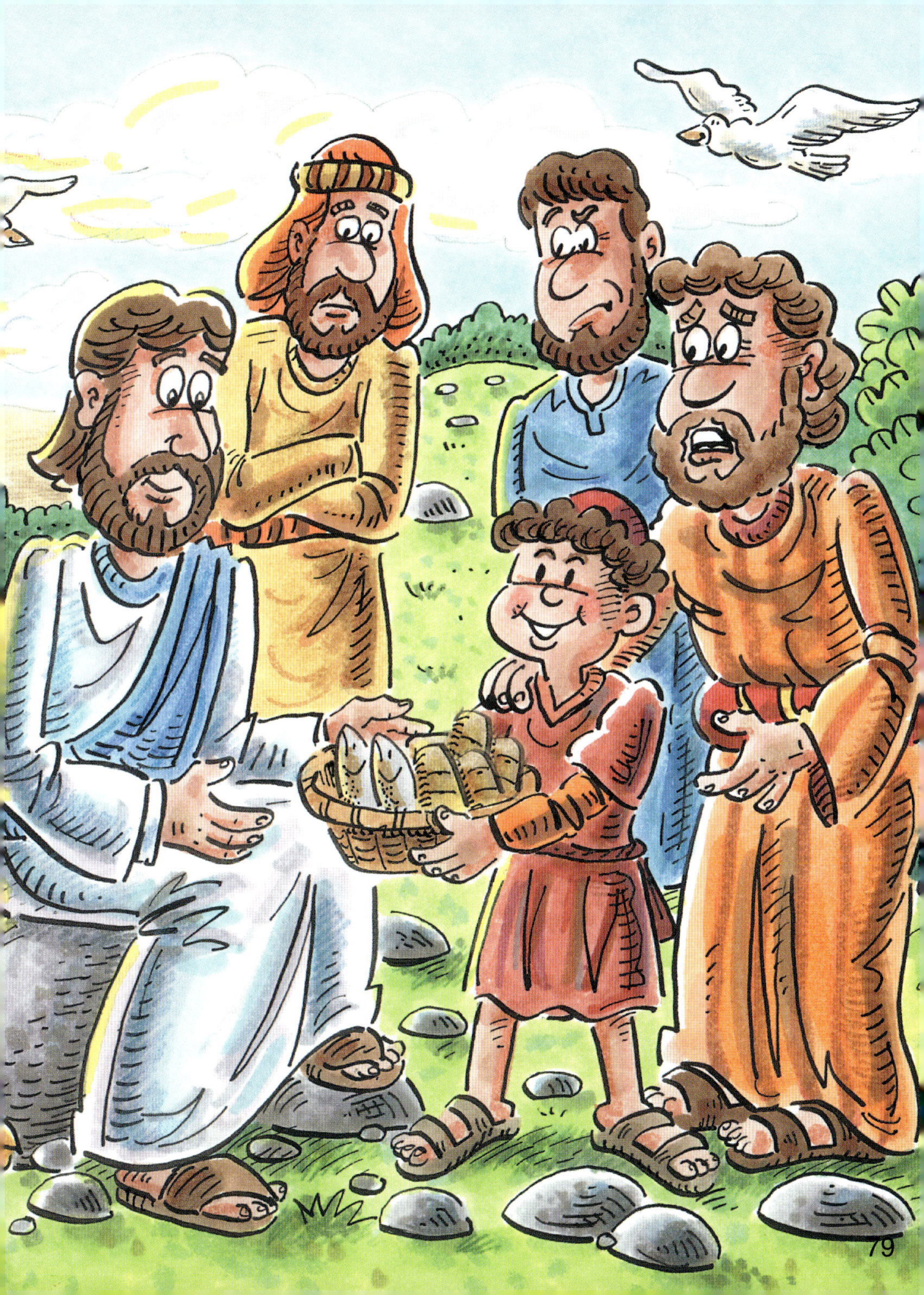

Then Jesus spoke, "Bring it to Me;
Seat people on the ground."
He took the food and then gave thanks
And handed it around.

Each lady, man, and child, in turn,
Took some and passed it on.
They ate and ate and ate lots more.
The food still was not gone.

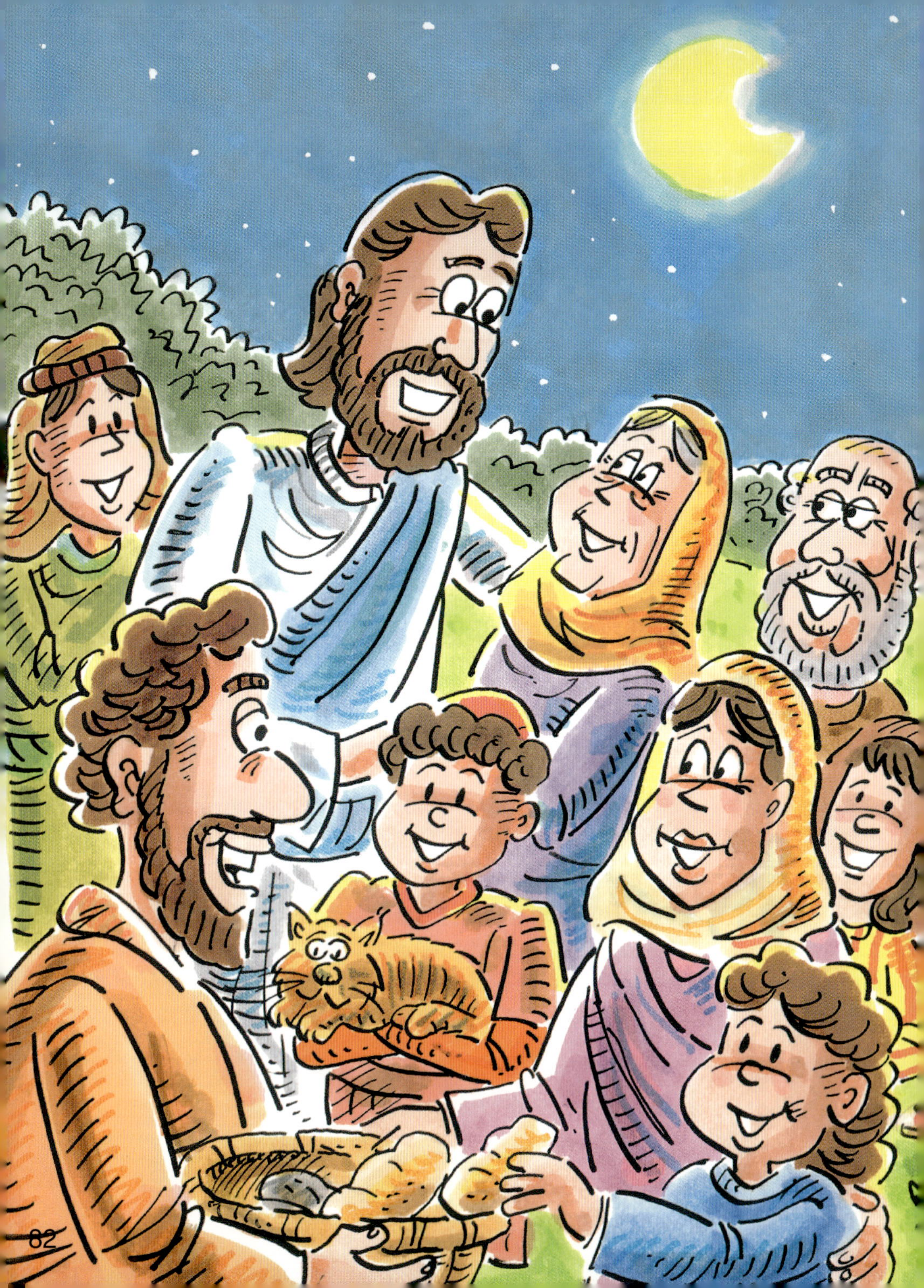

Now Jesus gave them this command,
"You've had enough to eat,
So gather pieces that are left
Of barley loaves and meat."

They filled 12 baskets with the crumbs
Too big to throw away.
Five thousand men plus moms and kids
Were fed by God that day.

God cares for us as He did them.
He gives us all we need.
He blesses us with food and drink.
These gifts are guaranteed.

Let's thank our God as Jesus did
And bow our heads to pray.
We'll ask Him for His blessing now
For each and every day.

Dear Jesus, bless Your little child
And care for me each day.
Please be with me and use my gifts
To serve in my own way.

Dear Parents:

You may want to spread a blanket on the floor and enjoy a "picnic" while reading this book with your child. Talk about the joy the little boy must have felt in being able to share his lunch with Jesus. Explain that Jesus takes our small gifts and uses them to do great things. The offerings we give at church help people around the world come to know their Savior. The loving things we do to help one another reflect God's great love in sending His Son to die for us.

Plan a way that you and your child can share Jesus' love. Donate food to your church's food pantry or a homeless shelter. Visit a lonely neighbor or relative. Take cookies or dinner to someone who has been ill or is in the midst of moving. Thank Jesus for blessing your small gift of love with His great love.

The Editor

Jesus Wakes the Little Girl

The story of Jairus's daughter

Matthew 9:18–19, 23–26; Mark 5:21–24, 35–43; and Luke 8:40–42, 49–56 for children

Written by Joanne Bader

Illustrated by Michelle Dorenkamp

One day when Jesus took a boat
To go across the sea,
A large crowd waited on the shore
In nearby Galilee.

They welcomed Him when He arrived.
They were expecting Him,
When suddenly a man appeared
Whose face looked very grim.

This man, who ruled the synagogue,
Had "Jairus" as his name.
He fell right down at Jesus' feet
To tell just why he came.

"My only daughter, twelve years old,
Is near to death," he said.
"Please come and lay Your hands on her
So she will live instead!"

Now Jesus went along with him
And the disciples too.
The whole crowd followed close behind
To see what He would do.

So Jairus led them to his house—
He was in a hurry.
He had great faith in Jesus' pow'r.
He tried not to worry.

Along the way there came a man
Who then to Jairus said,
"The Teacher is not needed for
Your daughter now is dead!"

But Jesus overheard his words
And told the ruler then,
"You must not fear. Only believe—
She will be well again."

When they got to the ruler's house,
They could hear loud weeping.
But Jesus said, "She is not dead.
She is only sleeping."

The mourners there all laughed at Him,
For they knew she was dead.
They'd all been right inside the house—
Some very near her bed.

Then Jesus sent the crowd away,
And when they all were gone,
He took her mom and dad inside
With Peter, James, and John.

98

He held her hand and said to her,
"Now, little girl, arise!"
And she got up and walked around
Before their wondering eyes.

"Get her some food, for she must eat,"
That's just what Jesus said.
And all the people gathered there
Could see she was not dead.

Jesus is God! He raised the girl!
Her parents were amazed.
They knew it was a miracle.
They thanked Him and they praised.

Their little girl was well again.
She now had life and breath,
And she could run and talk and play.
Jesus had conquered death.

As Jesus rose from His own death,
We, too, will rise someday.
And we will go to heaven with Him
Who took our sins away.

Dear Parents,

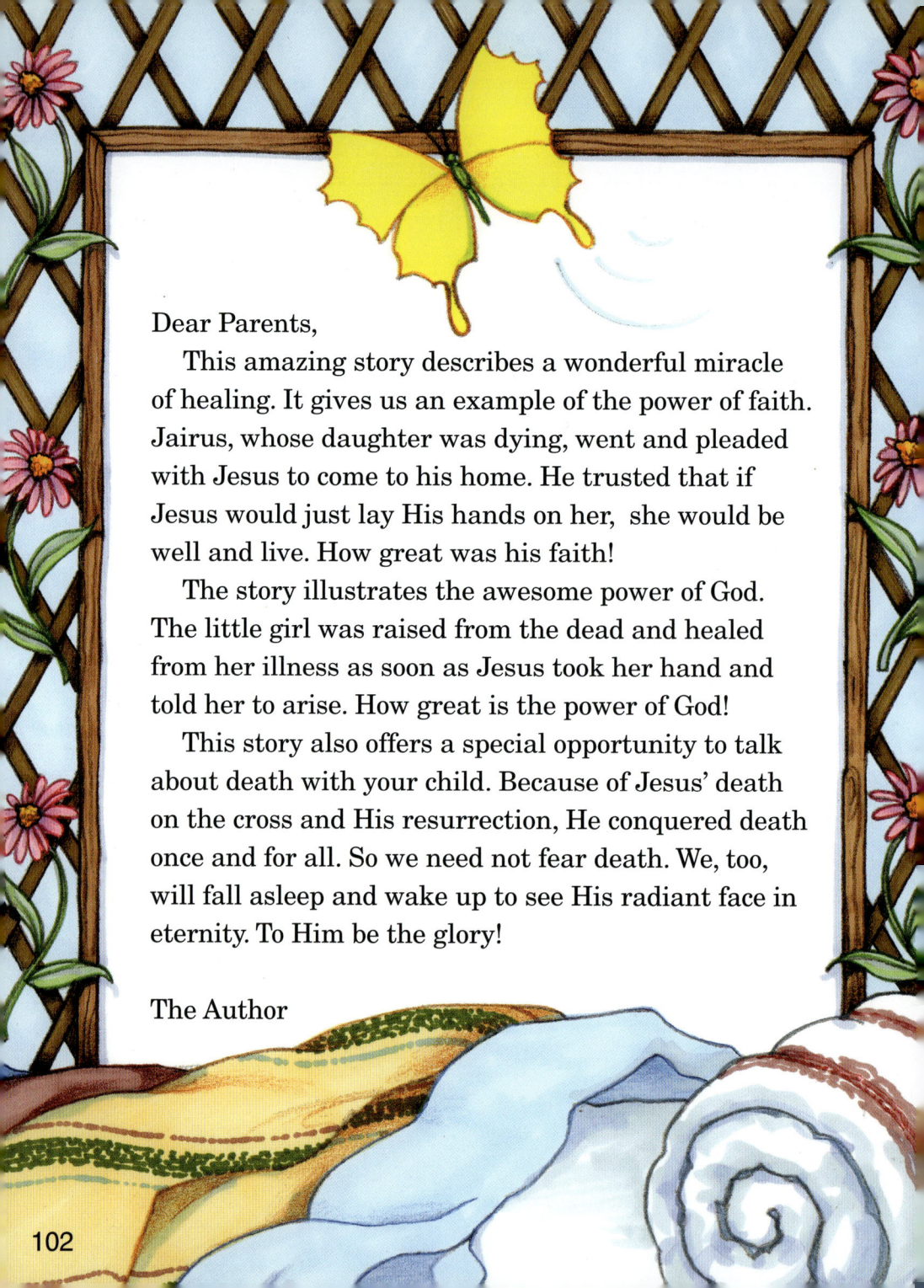

   This amazing story describes a wonderful miracle of healing. It gives us an example of the power of faith. Jairus, whose daughter was dying, went and pleaded with Jesus to come to his home. He trusted that if Jesus would just lay His hands on her, she would be well and live. How great was his faith!

   The story illustrates the awesome power of God. The little girl was raised from the dead and healed from her illness as soon as Jesus took her hand and told her to arise. How great is the power of God!

   This story also offers a special opportunity to talk about death with your child. Because of Jesus' death on the cross and His resurrection, He conquered death once and for all. So we need not fear death. We, too, will fall asleep and wake up to see His radiant face in eternity. To Him be the glory!

The Author

The Arch® Book Bible Story Library

Bible Beginnings

59-1577	The Fall into Sin
59-1534	The First Brothers
59-2206	A Man Named Noah
59-1511	Noah's 2-by-2 Adventure
59-1560	The Story of Creation
59-2239	Where Did the World Come From?

The Old Testament

59-1502	Abraham's Big Test
59-2244	Abraham, Sarah, and Isaac
59-2229	Daniel and the Lions
59-1559	David and Goliath
59-1593	David and His Friend Jonathan
59-2220	Deborah Saves the Day
59-1543	Elijah Helps the Widow
59-2251	Ezekiel and the Dry Bones
59-1567	The Fiery Furnace
59-1570	God Calls Abraham . . . God Calls You!
59-1587	God Provides Victory through Gideon
59-1523	God's Fire for Elijah
59-1542	Good News for Naaman
59-2223	How Enemies Became Friends
59-2247	Isaac Blesses Jacob and Esau
59-1538	Jacob's Dream
59-1539	Jericho's Tumbling Walls
59-2246	Jonah, the Runaway Prophet
59-1514	Jonah and the Very Big Fish
59-2233	Joseph, Jacob's Favorite Son
59-2216	King Josiah and God's Book
59-1583	The Lord Calls Samuel
59-2219	Moses and the Bronze Snake
59-1607	Moses and the Long Walk
59-2266	The Mystery of the Moving Hand
59-1535	A Mother Who Prayed
59-2249	One Boy, One Stone, One God
59-2253	Queen Esther Visits the King
59-2211	Ruth and Naomi
59-2276	Samson
59-1586	The Ten Commandments
59-1608	The Ten Plagues
59-2263	The Tower of Babel
59-1550	Tiny Baby Moses
59-1530	Tried and True Job
59-2260	The 23rd Psalm
59-1603	Zerubbabel Rebuilds the Temple

The New Testament

59-1580	The Coming of the Holy Spirit
59-2259	The Great Commission
59-2207	His Name Is John
59-1532	Jailhouse Rock
59-1520	Jesus and the Family Trip
59-2277	Jesus and the Rich Young Man
59-1588	Jesus Calls His Disciples
59-2215	Jesus Shows His Glory
59-2270	Lydia Believes
59-1521	Mary and Martha's Dinner Guest
59-2269	Nicodemus and Jesus
59-2227	Paul's Great Basket Caper
59-2267	The Pentecost Story
59-1578	Philip and the Ethiopian
59-1601	Saul's Conversion
59-1574	Timothy Joins Paul
59-2222	Twelve Ordinary Men
59-1599	Zacchaeus

Arch® Book Companions

59-2232	The Fruit of the Spirit
59-1609	God, I've Gotta Talk to You
59-1575	The Lord's Prayer
59-1562	My Happy Birthday Book
59-2271	Best-Loved Christmas Stories
59-2272	Best-Loved Parables of Jesus
59-2273	Best-Loved Miracles of Jesus
59-2274	Best-Loved Easter Stories

Christmas Arch® Books

59-1579	Baby Jesus Is Born
59-1544	Baby Jesus Visits the Temple
59-1553	Born on Christmas Morn
59-2261	The Christmas Angels
59-1605	The Christmas Message
59-2225	The Christmas Promise
59-1546	Joseph's Christmas Story
59-1499	Mary's Christmas Story
59-1584	My Merry Christmas Arch® Book
59-2252	Oh, Holy Night!
59-1537	On a Silent Night
59-2243	Once Upon a Clear Dark Night
59-2234	The Shepherds Shook in Their Shoes
59-2268	The Songs of Christmas
59-1594	Star of Wonder
59-2209	When Jesus Was Born

Easter Arch® Books

59-1551	Barabbas Goes Free
59-2205	The Centurion at the Cross
59-1516	The Day Jesus Died
59-2213	The Easter Gift
59-2221	The Easter Stranger
59-2275	The Easter Surprise
59-1602	The Easter Victory
59-2265	From Adam to Easter
59-1582	Good Friday
59-1585	Jesus Enters Jerusalem
59-1561	Jesus Returns to Heaven
59-2248	John's Easter Story
59-1592	Mary Magdalene's Easter Story
59-1564	My Happy Easter Arch® Book
59-2258	The Gardens of Easter
59-2231	The Resurrection
59-1517	The Story of the Empty Tomb
59-1504	Thomas, the Doubting Disciple
59-1501	The Very First Lord's Supper
59-1541	The Week That Led to Easter

Parables and Lessons of Jesus

59-2257	Jesus and the Canaanite Woman
59-1589	Jesus and the Woman at the Well
59-1500	Jesus Blesses the Children
59-1595	Jesus, My Good Shepherd
59-2245	Jesus Teaches Us Not to Worry
59-1540	Jesus Washes Peter's Feet
59-2264	The Lesson of the Tree and Its Fruit
59-1606	The Lost Coin
59-2235	The Parable of the Ten Bridesmaids
59-2218	The Parable of the Lost Sheep
59-2224	The Parable of the Prodigal Son
59-2262	The Parable of the Seeds
59-2210	The Parable of the Talents
59-2254	The Parable of the Woman and the Judge
59-2250	The Parable of the Workers in the Vineyard
59-1512	The Seeds That Grew and Grew
59-1503	The Story of Jesus' Baptism and Temptation
59-1596	The Story of the Good Samaritan
59-2214	The Widow's Offering
59-2208	The Wise and Foolish Builders

Miracles Jesus Performed

59-1531	Down through the Roof
59-1568	Get Up, Lazarus!
59-1604	The Great Catch of Fish
59-1581	Jesus Calms the Storm
59-1598	Jesus' First Miracle
59-2230	Jesus Heals Blind Bartimaeus
59-2255	Jesus Heals the Man at the Pool
59-2236	Jesus Heals the Centurion's Servant
59-2226	Jesus Wakes the Little Girl
59-1597	Jesus Walks on the Water
59-1558	A Meal for Many
59-2212	The Thankful Leper
59-1510	What's for Lunch